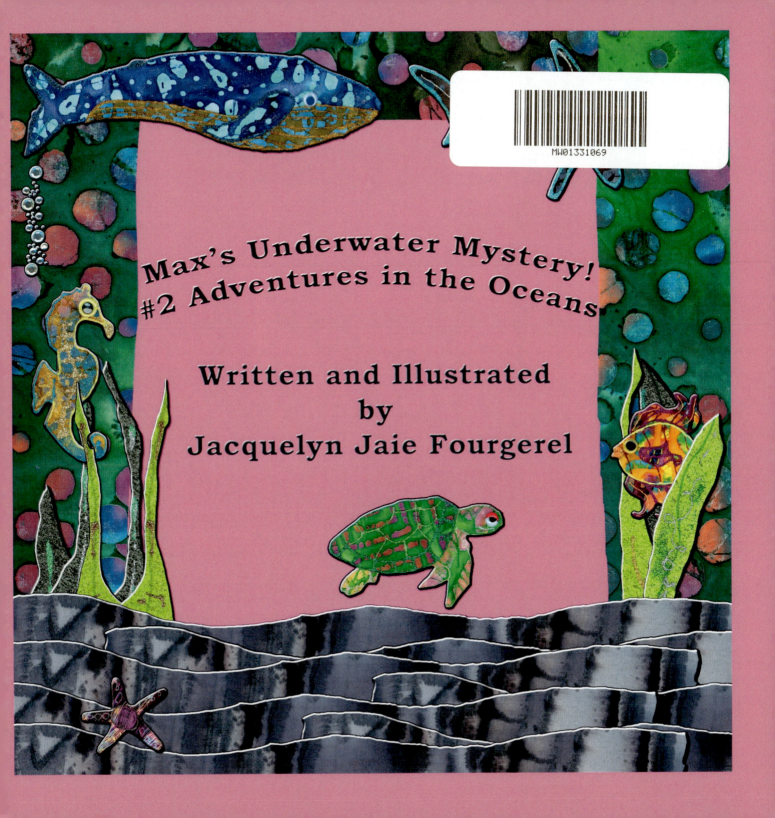

Max's Underwater Mystery!
#2 Adventures in the Oceans

Written and Illustrated
by
Jacquelyn Jaie Fourgerel

"Dad! Mom! I am going out to find more underwater mysteries. See you later!" screamed Max, his voice full of adventure.

"OK! Have fun and enjoy exploring those underwater mysteries," Mom said.

But Max had left the seaweed home before he heard what his mom said.

"Are you an underwater mystery?" Max asked.

"Yes, I am an underwater mystery. I am an aggressive hunter, and…

"Are you an underwater mystery?" Max asked.

"Yes, I am an underwater mystery. I have a large hard shell that protects my body, but…

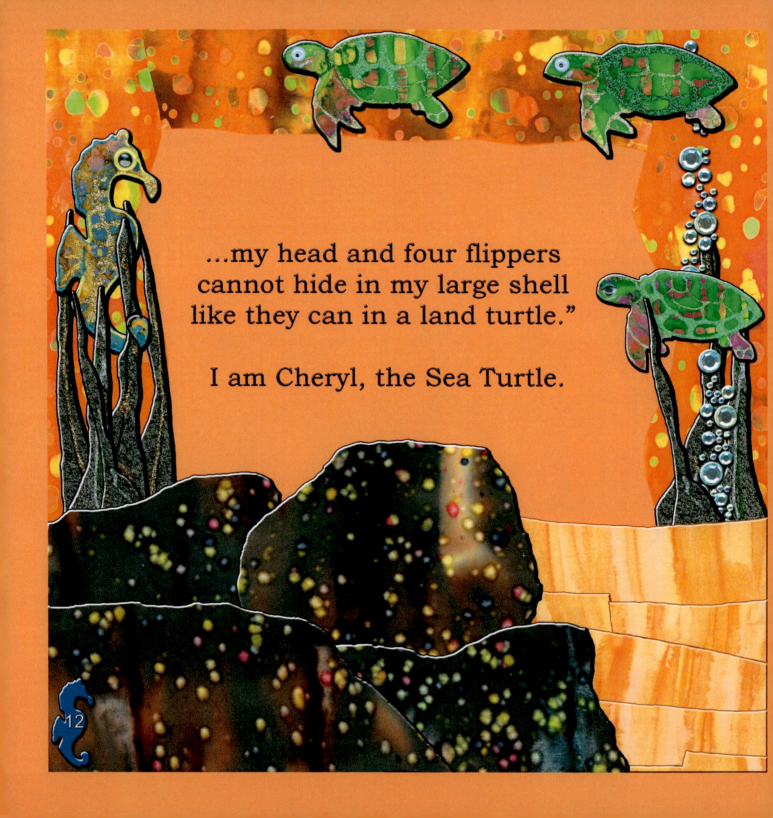

"...my head and four flippers cannot hide in my large shell like they can in a land turtle."

I am Cheryl, the Sea Turtle.

..."I outnumber all the other animals on Earth, which include amphibians, birds, mammals, and reptiles - all put together."

I am Christina, the Tropical Fish.

"Are you an underwater mystery?" Max asked.

"Yes, I am an underwater mystery. I am the largest animal in the world, and…

…I can grow to 100 feet and can weigh 180 tons.
I am on the endangered list!"

I am Kevin, the Blue Whale.

"Are you an underwater mystery?" Max asked.

"Yes, I am an underwater mystery. I can have 5 to 50 arms. I do not have any blood; instead I pump sea water up through my legs, and...

...many call me starfish but my real name is Sea Star or Spiny Skin."

I am Jacquelyn, the Sea Star.

"Dad! Mom! Do you know what? I am an underwater mystery, too!" excitedly Max announced when he entered his seaweed house.

"Yes you are an underwater mystery, my son!" Mom replied.

"What did you learned about yourself, today?" Dad asked.

"I have no scales; instead I am a bony fish with a thin skin to cover my exoskeleton. I have great eyesight and my eyes can look at two different objects at the same time. My long snout helps me to find food in nooks and crannies!" Max exclaimed.

"Wow! That is a lot of knowledge that you learned today. What do you think you are going too learned tomorrow?" Mom asked Max.

But Max fell asleep before he could answer.

Sea Creatures

The Blue whale can live for 40 years, grow to 100 ft. and weigh up to 180 tons! There are about 12,000 blue whales living today in the ocean. An adult blue whale eats 40 million krill in a day. The blue whale can stay underwater for one hour before surfacing for air.

The Hammerhead shark can live for 30 years, grow to 20 ft. and weigh up to 1,300 lbs. They have a blind spot right in front of their noses but can see very well. All sharks can pick up electricity from all living things, which helps them hunt or get away from danger.

The Seahorse can live for 5 years, grow to 14 in., and weigh up to 2 lbs. The word seahorse comes from the Greek word hippocampus, which means (hippo-horse) and (campus-sea monster). Seahorses bond in pairs for life. A baby seahorse is called a fry. Seahorses have a swim bladder and breathe with gills.

The Sea star can live for 35 years, grow to 9.5 in. and weigh up to 11 lbs. The starfish are not real fish and their true name is Sea Star or Spiny Skin. They do not have eyes; they have eyespots that detect light and darkness.

The Sea turtle can live for 150 years, grow to 8 ft. and weigh up to 2,000 lbs. They can travel very long distances to find their food. Sea turtles live in the oceans' continental shelves all over the world. They nest in tropical areas.

The Tropical fish can live for 20 years and come in all different shapes, sizes, and colors. Some tropical fish have lungs and can breathe air from the surface, while others have only gills to breathe underwater.

Dedication:

Christina Fourgerel and Dan Bogert

Acknowledgement:

Thank you to Susan Fourgerel and Gerri Post who helped edit this book.

About the Author:

Jacquelyn received her B.S. in Psychology from the UMass, Amherst and her M.S. in Childhood Education and Childhood Special Education from LIU.

Other Books:

Butterfly Haiku

Max's Underwater Mystery! #1: Exploring the Oceans

Underwater Mystery Haiku #1

Contact: jfourgerel@gmail.com

Website: jacquelynjaiefourgerel.com

Max's Underwater Mystery! # 2: Adventures in the Oceans

Written and Illustrated by Jacquelyn Jaie Fourgerel

Copyright: 2014 Jacquelyn Jaie Fourgerel. All Rights Reserved.

Technical and Graphic Editing by: Susan Fourgerel

ISBN-13: 978-1517449254

ISBN-10: 1517449251

Printed by: CreateSpace an Amazon Company 2015

No part of this book may be reproduced, stored in a retrieval system, or transmitted by any means without the written permission of the author.

"Hope you join me on my next adventure exploring the oceans' sea creatures!

Max's Underwater Mystery! # 3: Traveling the Oceans.

See you soon!"